the SIX
QUESTIONS

the SIX QUESTIONS

That You Better Get Right
The Answers are the Keys to Your Success

Workbook

JULIE EDMONDS & MICHELL SMITH

NEW YORK

the SIX QUESTIONS

That You Better Get Right The Answers are the Keys to Your Success

ISBN 9781614483359 paperback
Library of Congress Control Number: 2012935390

Morgan James Publishing
The Entrepreneurial Publisher
5 Penn Plaza, 23rd Floor, New York City, New York 10001
(212) 655-5470 office • (516) 908-4496 fax
www.MorganJamesPublishing.com

In an effort to support local communities, raise awareness and funds, Morgan James Publishing donates a percentage of all book sales for the life of each book to Habitat for Humanity Peninsula and Greater Williamsburg.

Get involved today, visit
www.MorganJamesBuilds.com.

Habitat for Humanity®
Peninsula and
Greater Williamsburg
Building Partner

TABLE OF CONTENTS

INTRODUCTION

As a woman in a man's world, learning to navigate the realm of business and leadership was comparable to charting a course to a yet undiscovered planet in another solar system. Starting out as young entrepreneurs, business success was something we both yearned for, however, knowing what to do and figuring out what route to take was a guessing game. It was a guessing game until we discovered *the Six Questions*.

Now before we even get to *the Six Questions*, we have some very important issues to address particularly with women that we sometimes sabotage ourselves with. The odds are that we put ourselves last. The odds are that we believe being a woman will make it harder for us to succeed. The odds are that we feel guilty and consider it selfish to take care of ourselves at times. The odds are that we feel we need someone else to make us feel loved. The odds are that we feel unappreciated by some people in our lives and we allow this to deflate us... We need to make the odds even, before we can properly begin.

MAKING THE ODDS EVEN...

(This part's for the girls)

How the battle is won...

Chapter 1

WE WANT IT ALL

We do want it all. The feelings we crave ... when our hearts feel that they could beat straight out of our chests, and that deep connectedness that we long for in all of the things in our lives: the passion of love, the warmth of friendship, the fulfillment of contribution and the joy of accomplishment; the seduction of attraction and the thrill of excitement. We want to feel them all.

Our Challenge

The challenge is that as women we have a high desire for feeling fulfilled. We map our lives by how we feel and how we want to feel. When we turn off emotionally we begin to make decisions outside ourselves, living on autopilot on a safe, pre-selected route until we can handle driving again. Some of us don't go through this as dramatically, but for others ... we get really good at believing that we are just ... fine.

We do want it all, and I am not talking about material things, positions or titles but the real truth that lies in every one of us--to feel loved and important, successful and sexy, attractive and appreciated, treasured, protected, safe ... and still free.

Odds are we don't spend enough time even thinking about this. Odds are, we spend more time thinking about what everybody else in our lives wants and needs, and we use our ability to help them get it as the gauge to determine our own value.

That's just plain wrong.

I, _____ , recognize that I need to make the odds even for myself and my life.

Ways that I need to do this are:

_____

_____

_____

_____

_____

_____

_____

_____

_____

_____

_____

_____

_____

_____

_____

_____

_____

_____

_____

_____

_____

_____

_____

_____

_____

_____

_____

_____

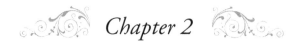

Chapter 2

THE X FACTOR

The *X Factor* holds the key...

The X Factor--Immeasurable self love. The love we have available for others is limitless. The depth of the love that we have for a child is indescribably, consumingly, painfully, overwhelmingly all encompassing ... an actual physical presence of power. The love we have available for ourselves is this exact same love. Our capacity is endless.

We attain the power of the X Factor only when we learn to allow this love also to grow *for ourselves*. This is when we become not an object of love, but a manufacturing plant of lovingness for our own lives and the fortunate ones that we fill our lives with.

In business, choosing to play ball with the big boys, as a woman, brings with it a certain risk. You have to feel genuinely confident about who you are already and the abilities you have; learning to navigate the corporate battlefield as a woman is no easy task, and it's nobody else's responsibility to make it easier for you.

We made so many changes as we grew up through our careers in order to see ourselves as strong business people. We wore pantsuits and ponytails, dark colors and high collared shirts, carried big briefcases and left the perfume at home....

It didn't much matter. That's when we realized that no one else determines our ability to succeed --we do. How we honestly feel about ourselves is the biggest driver of our results. Add that to commitment and performance, and then we actually have a shot at being a player. So, we don't dress in grey in order to blend in and not be seen as women any more.... If they're going to imagine us naked, they're going to do it anyways.

Ways that I will embrace my own X Factor are:

_____

_____

_____

_____

_____

_____

_____

_____

_____

_____

_____

_____

_____

_____

_____

_____

_____

_____

_____

_____

_____

_____

_____

_____

Making the odds even means truly embracing our assets as wonderful, capable women. We are not the weaker sex, not emotionally or intuitively, not from a mental strength perspective or a capability perspective. We must stop permitting any thinking that being female somehow prevents us. It's our own thinking this that creates this as a reality.

THE SIX QUESTIONS

Each of these questions must be asked and answered honestly, before you move on to the next one. If you do not like an answer, learn to change it. Getting the right answers to these questions is required; getting them wrong carries too high a price.

But before you get started, quickly come visit us for a warm welcome from Julie and Michell.

**Scan the code or visit the link @
www.julieandmichell.com/ launch_welcome.html**

CLARITY

Question Number One:
HOW CLEAR ARE YOU ON WHAT YOU WANT?

Knowing the answer to this question with complete clarity is like enabling the missile lock on a high-powered weapon of overwhelming capability.

> "Happiness comes when
> you believe in what you are doing,
> know what you are doing,
> and love what you are doing."
> -*Brian Tracy*

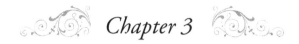
GETTING CLARITY

The Five Steps

Step 1: *Slow down and clear your mind.*

Begin with a meditation:

Take deep breaths, and take some quiet time for yourself.

This will help you clear your head and let your heart speak to you.

When our minds are free from the clutter, it's easy to hear our heart speak.

Take 10 deep breathes with your eyes closed.

Clear your mind and let go of anything that is bothering you.

Let your mind just relax.

Think of every deep breath as revitalizing your body.

Breath out any worries, concerns, issues,....

Allow your mind to fantasize about the life you want.

Smile.

Now think of a bigger and better more loving place than before and more peaceful. Smile.

Keep going.

Allow your heart to fill you with joy and hope.

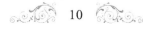

What things are you visualizing?
What places did you go to?
Who was with you?

_____

_____

_____

_____

_____

_____

Step 2: *Define the "why's".*

Understanding how to be clear on what's right for us is part of designing and redesigning our lives. One of the easiest ways to figure out what's right for you is to figure out the "why's" behind what you are seeking.

- Why do I want to ?
- Why do I want to ?
- Why do I want to?
- Why do I want to?

_____

_____

_____

_____

_____

_____

Step 3: *Find your purpose.*

_____

_____

_____

_____

_____

_____

Step 4: *Identify the fear.*

To understand our own belief systems, get clarity on what we truly want, and decide who we truly are, follow the next steps. Answer as honestly as possible without over-thinking it.

1. Decide what you want to **become** rather that what you **want**. (It's best to keep this part as general as possible and list as many as you can that come to mind.)

I want to **become**:

_____
_____

I want to **become**:

_____
_____

I want to **become**:

_____
_____

2. Next to each answer above, answer **why, along with the feeling it brings.**
Example: I want to **become** a *reputable person in my community* because it **(why)** *gives me purpose, freedom, and challenge* and I **feel (feeling)** *worthy.*

Fill in the blank: I want to **become** a _____ because it
(why) _____
and I **feel (feeling)** _____

Fill in the blank: I want to **become** a _____ because it
(why) _____
and I **feel (feeling)** _____

Fill in the blank: I want to **become** a _____ because it
(why) _____
and I **feel (feeling)** _____

3. Define the **FEAR** that you may feel if you do not achieve your **why. Also define the fear that may be stopping you from achieving your "why".**

Example: If I don't have **(why)** *purpose, freedom, and challenge in life,* I **(fear)** *I will be lost, trapped, constricted, bored or overworked.*

Fill in the blanks:

If I don't have **(why)** _____

I **(fear)** _____

If I don't have **(why)** _____

I **(fear)** _____

If I don't have **(why)** _____

I **(fear)** _____

4. List all the whys and feelings you stated above in number 2. And list all your fears you stated in number 3.

For example:

WHYS: Purpose, Freedom, Challenge

FEELINGS: Worthy

FEARS: Lost, Trapped, Constricted, Overworked

WHYS: _____

_____

_____

FEELINGS: _____

_____

_____

FEARS: _____

_____

_____

> The way you feel about something or the fear it entails are powerful driving forces of your actions and choices.

Step 5: *Make a list:*

Remember Your Five Steps

STEP 1 on Getting Clear: *Slow down and clear your mind.*

STEP 2 on Getting Clear: *Define your "whys" behind what you are seeking.*

STEP 3 on Getting Clear: *Find your purpose.*

STEP 4 on Getting Clear: *Identify the fear associated with your desires; learn to transcend them.*

STEP 5 on Getting Clear: *Smile and start making a long list of everything you deserve.*

Chapter 4

CHECKOUT LINE

In fnding the answer to the first question, it's important to weigh and measure the consequences of what we are asking for.

Life's Shopping List

This is the most important shopping list you will ever make. It is not a static list, it will change many many times throughout your life, just as any shopping list will change---different grocery list for a week in your 20's than what will be on that list when you are 50! You do not make this list once in your life, and it is not a list that you commit to – this is a list that frees you. Take the time to write down with reckless abandon everything that comes to mind that you would like to do or be or have in your life. You can write down things with a question mark too that you want to look into. The intent with this process is to look at everything that is on your list at the same time!

    Go For It – Get Crazy!!

Things I want to do, Things I want to be, Things I want to have:

_____

_____

_____

_____

_____

When I was a child I dreamed of:

_____
_____
_____
_____

In high-school I wanted to:

_____
_____
_____
_____

I thought about studying:

_____
_____
_____
_____

In college/university I played with the idea of:

_____
_____
_____
_____

My friends always said I should:

_____
_____
_____
_____

If money wasn't an object then I would:

_____
_____
_____
_____

After I

_____

_____

_____

THEN I will:

_____

_____

_____

_____

_____

_____

The Truest Guides:

Question 1: How do I feel right now?

_____

_____

_____

Question 2: How do I want to feel?

_____

_____

_____

Question 3: What will make me feel this way?

_____

_____

_____

> "You have to pay the price. You will find that everything in life exacts a price, and you will have to decide whether the price is worth the prize."
> *-Sam Nunn*

The Price of What's On Our Lists:

When we make certain choices it's important to be aware that we are also choosing to pay the price that comes with those choices--not only financial prices, but costs to relationships, health and wellness, dreams and happiness and time with loved ones. These are the real payments that we make through our lives.

Life's Shopping List and Price Guide

Things		Price
	=	
	=	
	=	
	=	
	=	
	=	
	=	
	=	
	=	
	=	
	=	

What prices are acceptable and what prices are unacceptable? What should we remove from our list if anything and what should we focus on first?

The Underlying WHY?

To help ensure that our choices are on the right track we are now trained to go deeper than the first "why?" We learned this through the wisdom of the four-year-olds in this world and their commitment to the "Why?" game.

Lets Play! Look back at your Life's Shopping List and see if there are items on that list that are competing with each other. Sometimes this happens and we get to choose what first! Not which one, but - which one first? Deciding which one first can be easier if you play the why game with your list:

I want to:

_____

_____

_____

Why?

_____

_____

_____

Why?

_____

_____

_____

Why?

_____

_____

_____

Why?

_____

_____

_____

Get to the bottom of your real reasons. Integrity with your intention is a driving force behind action.

19

> Understand what you will trade for what you decide to pursue, and understand what you will give up for what you don't--your happiness depends on this.

What I want:

_____
_____
_____

Different ways to get this are:

_____
_____
_____

The first steps for now are:

_____
_____
_____

> Have the wisdom of a fisherman...

- What do you want?
- What makes you happy?
- What makes you happiest?
- If life could be exactly as you want it--what would that look like?
- Will your list of choices and the prices you agree to pay get you this life?

> Build a relationship with your future.

It takes fierce courage to do this. Admitting what you want can be scary. There is a reason why studies show that only three percent of us actually even get this far and answer question number one. Ninety seven percent of us never do. Ninety seven percent of us do not make a decision and write down our goals; Ninety seven percent of us think it is too much work to even think about....

More people go to psychics and fortune tellers to ask what's in store for their future than people who actually decide on their future and set goals for themselves. Doesn't this seem irresponsible? Yes!

> "I read once that 99 percent of all people give up on their goals before they even start. That struck me as a bit sad, and perhaps this has been the truth historically. **Accepting that this is the rule seems reckless.** We should change that statistic together. Perhaps that's the way it used to be, but with all of the education and awareness, strength and potential that exists in all of us we should "stale date" that statistic, and change it to teach the generations of the future."
> *-Michell*

The reason they give up is because they don't use *the Six Questions* to guide them. They are not clear on what they want, they are not committed, or they are not confident. Using *the Six Questions* to guide you will give you the awareness you need to part of the 1%.

I, _____, on this _____ day of _____ 201__, do solemnly swear to be part of the 1%, and accept the challenge to change this statistic for generations of the future. I will keep my Life's Shopping List as my map for the future and live a life that I love.

Signed: _____

Witnessed: _____

The price of not going after what you want is often times higher than the price would have been to get it. This is not a practice life. A price gets paid for all choices, whether they are choices to take action or choices not to.

"I believe in crystal balls. But the crystal balls I believe in are the ones you can grow yourself--with courage and decision, awareness, and industrious work ethic. You decide what you want in the future and you work on getting it. How well your crystal balls work, at accurately seeing your future ... that all depends on you, and how you answer *the Six Questions*."
-Michell

Rate yourself from 1 – 10 with 1 being unclear and 10 being clear:

How Clear are you right now? _____

How Clear do you want to be? _____

CLARITY LEADS TO COMMITMENT

Question Number Two:
HOW COMMITTED ARE YOU TO GETTING IT?

99 percent committed is not enough.

> "Courage is the commitment to begin w
> ithout any guarantee of success."
> *-Johann Wolfgang Von Goethe*

Chapter 5

COURAGE, CONVICTION, & COMMITMENT

FEAR: How do I define fear?

_____

_____

_____

_____

What fears are stopping you?

_____

_____

_____

_____

_____

What are some current fears that you have that you feel are holding you back?

_____

_____

_____

_____

Courage

1. What are some things I would really like to do, but I am terrified to do them?

_____
_____
_____
_____
_____
_____
_____
_____
_____

2. What are some things I really would like to ask for, but I am afraid of the potential outcomes?

_____
_____
_____
_____
_____
_____
_____
_____

3. What are some things that I really need to do, but I am fearful of the change?

_____
_____
_____
_____
_____
_____
_____

Study the diagram and fill in the areas that are comfortable and uncomfortable to you with each bubble.

With each section, what is outside of your comfort zone?

Social _____
_____

Career _____
_____

Financial _____
_____

Health _____
_____

How committed are you to getting what you want?

The truest test to your commitment is your ability to transcend your fear in any area.

On a scale from one to ten, (Ten being an absolute must and one being something you can live with without much loss) Rate each section on how badly you want to transcend the fear.

Social   1 2 3 4 5 6 7 8 9 10

Career   1 2 3 4 5 6 7 8 9 10

Financial   1 2 3 4 5 6 7 8 9 10

Health   1 2 3 4 5 6 7 8 9 10

Start with the highest numbers first and work backwards:

Ask yourself these questions:
What has to happen to accomplish this?

What are you willing to do to get it?

Who can hold you accountable?

_____

_____

_____

_____

_____

Conviction & Commitment
Conviction is the complete belief that you can make something happen because you believe it from the bottom of your heart.

I _____, commit with all of my heart and soul,
to _____ (Action) that will break comfort zone number _____
I will do it on this date _____ at this time _____

Signed: _____

Ask yourself these questions:
1. Am I 100% committed to my goal?

   _____
   _____

2. If not, what is holding me back?

   _____
   _____

3. What sacrifices am I willing to make in order to achieve my goal?

   _____
   _____

4. Do I believe that this can be accomplished, and can I speak with conviction about it?

   _____
   _____

5. Can I find the courage to make it happen?

   _____
   _____

6. Who can support me on this venture?

   _____
   _____

Integrity Check: Are my answers above the real truth?

_____
_____
_____
_____
_____

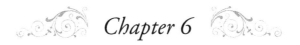

Chapter 6

BEWARE THE RECRUITERS

Decide who should be driving.

You operate best when you are in your mindset zone. Do your best to keep this zone as your "home base." This is a place that is inhabited by the set of emotions that are permitted to take your wheel. Happy, excited, thoughtful, confident--all of the best versions of you are grouped together holding down one entire quarter of your emotional wheel.

Put up barriers that act as buffers to keep you within this zone as much as possible by choice. To do this you must recruit for these emotions, and choose to do this daily. Some of these barriers are mental or internal decisions to think about the things you want to and to not think about the things you don't want to--others are barriers against certain people or negative influences in life surrounding you.

On the diagram below, draw a line on either side of the "zone" you want to live inside. Cross off any of the emotions that you do not want to have major influence on your daily life.

Emotions can be very dangerous. When they gain control it can feel like being intoxicated, or worse--possessed.

People in a rage are completely committed to that emotion. Rage is driving, navigating, targeting and destroying. Engaging in hostile, reactive activity with everyone it encounters, Rage is in complete control. We are not. Similarly, we have all done foolish things because we were in love! Think back to highs chool and recall a time when first you had feelings for someone, and how that COMPLETELY took over everything else in your ENTIRE world!!!!!!

Lets be truthful...
I make the best decisions when I'm feeling

_____

_____

I am the most productive when I'm feeling

_____

_____

I make bad or weak decisions when I'm feeling

_____

_____

I am the least productive when I'm feeling

_____

_____

I spend most of my time truthfully feeling

_____

_____

I need to spend more time feeling

_____

_____

And I need to spend less time feeling

_____

_____

...IF I WANT TO HAVE ANY CHANCE AT GETTING WHAT I REALLY WANT!

Things I need to stop doing to stop feeling the wrong way are:

_____

_____

Things I need to stop doing to stop feeling the wrong way are:

_____

_____

Things I need to stop doing to stop feeling the wrong way are:

_____

_____

Feeding the right emotions:

This is a choice we all consciously make – every single day of our lives. We are having an ongoing dialogue inside our minds with ourselves continuously (perhaps more chattier inside the minds of women!) We need to decisively fuel the emotions we yearn to feel.

The things that I've been blaming in my life that keep me feeling out of control, that I will no longer focus on , feed, or use as an excuse for the future are:

_____

_____

_____

_____

_____

Building the Other Side of Justice

What have I done, small or big, so far in my life that has allowed me to get this far that I can give myself credit for? What strengths do I have, what ethics and values have I lived by, what am I really proud of?

We all have a degree to which we allow ourselves to be emotional--an emotional volume setting of sorts. The degree to which we allow ourselves to become angered will echo the degree to which we allow ourselves to love, become sad, be excited, etc. Some of us are even turned completely off. Our emotional volume can be changed at any time by each of us; it is usually set to the level that feels right, however.

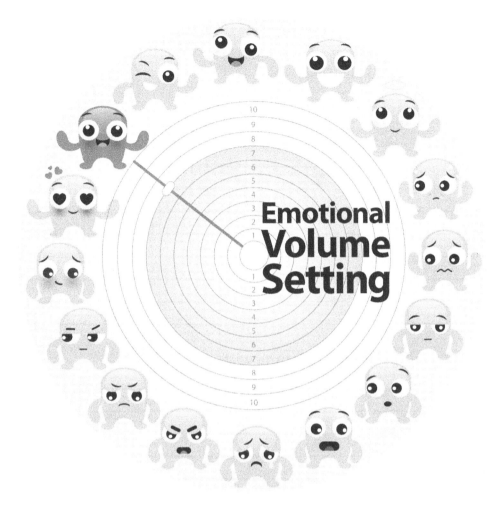

Make a note on this scale where you feel you live right now. Where would you like to live? Do you see how important it is to be in control if you plan to turn up the volume??

Things to consider...
When do we always turn down the volume???

I _____ resolve to always turn down the volume before making important decisions or having important discussions with people in my life, and _____ that I _____ which emotion is doing the driving.

Signed: _____ *Dated:* _____

Emotions have discovered that they stand a better chance at survival if they can control people collectively. They work as a unified force that attempts to gain strength through each of us. They spread throughout all of us and operate as a single entity.

Who else lives in your zone?

_____
_____
_____
_____
_____
_____
_____
_____

List the people you spend the most time with every day.

_____
_____
_____
_____
_____
_____
_____

List the other people who emotionally impact your life.

_____
_____
_____
_____
_____
_____

Draw below, with you in the centre and the other major people in your life as close to you as feels right, and way your emotional volumes overlap. Use the color that defines the feeling you believe each person is best represented by.

What do you think of the drawing?
How do these people make you feel?
How do these people feel themselves about their own lives?
What emotional volume are they set at?

How does this impact you?

_____
_____
_____
_____
_____
_____
_____
_____
_____
_____

Things I need to do are:

_____
_____
_____
_____
_____
_____
_____
_____

"When dealing with people remember you are not dealing with creatures of logic,
but with creatures of emotion, creatures bristling with prejudice,
and motivated by pride and vanity."
-Dale Carnegie

Chapter 7

PERFORMING THE EXORCISM

Committing yourself to getting what you want requires a removal of the negative energy that is stopping you from achieving your goals. Finding the right answer to question number two is fueled by this.

Gaining clarity through the emotional haze is necessary to make smart decisions. Any time you find yourself on the teeter totter of progress, go through this process.

Write down on paper the two sides which seem to be waging war inside of you, and all of their arguments. Give them their day in court. Examine all evidence and completely expose each side.

Then decide. Reach a verdict. Choose. Completely commit. One side wins, the other is silenced.

Ask yourself:
What decisions are haunting me right now?

_____

_____

_____

_____

_____

_____

_____

I need to figure out:

_____
_____
_____
_____
_____
_____
_____
_____

First I want to decide:

_____
_____
_____
_____
_____
_____

Everything I do not like about what I am currently doing; everything I am frustrated about having to tolerate or sacrifice while I choose to keep this in my life are:

_____
_____
_____
_____
_____
_____

Everything I do like about what I am doing right now and where it can bring me in the future:

_____
_____
_____
_____
_____
_____

Is it worth it to accept all of the above and continue? Yes or No

If you answered No, then what are you going to do next?

_____

_____

_____

_____

_____

_____

If you answered Yes then answer the following honestly:

The last time I put in 100% every day for 2 weeks straight was:

_____

_____

_____

I, _____ , understand that I will not make ANY progress on accomplishing what I want unless I put in _____ EVERY _____ UNTIL _____

_____

Signed: _____ *Dated:* _____

Are you clear on what you want? Are you committed to getting it? Then don't let anything stop you ... most of all, you.

Rate yourself from 1 – 10 with 1 being uncommitted and 10 being completely committed below:

How Committed have you been? _____

How Committed do you want to be? _____

How Committed are you right now? _____

CLARITY &
COMMITMENT
CREATES
CONFIDENCE

Question Number Three:

HOW DO YOU SEE YOURSELF?

How we see ourselves affects every single thing in our worlds.

> "Never doubt that you can change history.
> You already have."
> *-Marge Piercy*

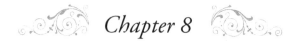
MIRROR, MIRROR ON THE WALL...

Define *luck*:

_____
_____
_____
_____
_____

What things have you been lucky with?

_____
_____
_____
_____
_____

The Prisoner

Description: This is an extreme mindset where we see ourselves as trapped and have zero control of our situation and our surroundings. Then we tend to start blaming everything and become unaccountable.

_____
_____

In what ways do you feel like a prisoner?

_____
_____
_____

What misfortune have you encountered that has changed the way you feel, see, or direct yourself?

_____
_____
_____
_____
_____
_____
_____

Do you ever find yourself thinking or saying these things:

Prisoner Statements:

1. No one cares.

   _____

   _____

2. I can't rely on anyone.

   _____

   _____

3. I always get the blame.

   _____

   _____

4. I am being targeted. They set me up to fail.

   _____

   _____

5. Things are so unfair.

   _____

   _____

6. They are all judging me.

   _____

   _____

What other Prisoner statements have you heard yourself say?

7. _____

   _____

8. _____

   _____

9. _____

   _____

10. _____

   _____

11. _____
    _____

12. _____
    _____

The Victor

Description: This is the other extreme mindset, where we can take full accountability for our mishaps and enjoy any success without fear that it is only a stroke of good luck.

_____
_____

In what ways do you feel like a Victor?

_____
_____

Victor Statements:
   1. I can handle it.

   _____
   _____

   2. I'll figure it out.

   _____
   _____

   3. I can approach this person or team without blame and get a different result.

   _____
   _____

   4. I can see myself in the other person's shoes.

   _____
   _____

   5. I am partly responsible.

   _____
   _____

Now fill in some of your own:

6. _____

_____

7. _____

_____

8. _____

_____

9. _____

_____

10. _____

_____

Prisoner vs Victor

Lets take a moment to acknowledge our participation when we are the prisoner and move the needle to Victor attitude: Using the diagram below think of a current situation where you are feeling conflict and mark on the scale where you see yourself.

◆   ◆   ◆   ◆   ◆   ◆

The Prisoner   The Victor

What can I do moving forward to get a different result than what is currently happening?

_____

_____

If I was in the persons shoes, what would I have done?

_____

_____

How can I approach this person or team without blame, to get a different result?

_____

_____

Am I the one that is causing the issue? What is my participation or involvement in it?

_____

_____

_____

_____

What responsible actions can I take or what other people can I delegate to?

_____

_____

_____

_____

I hold myself accountable for the team not getting the work done. What is my next step?

_____

_____

_____

What things can I control and what can I do moving forward?

_____

_____

_____

Where do I have to change my focus?

_____

_____

_____

I need to stop making assumptions about the person or circumstance and think to myself, what else did they mean?

_____

_____

_____

_____

When feeling like the prisoner or where your expectations are not being met, ask yourself these questions:

"What can I do about it?"

_____

_____

_____

_____

"How can I resolve this?"

_____

_____

_____

_____

"I can't change others, but I can change myself. How can I change myself or my approach, others will change the way they treat me?"

_____

_____

_____

_____

"The relationship has to work, I have to make this happen. What are my next steps?"

_____

_____

_____

_____

"What's the solution?"

_____

_____

_____

_____

"Is it really true what I'm thinking or did I make it up or overreact?"

_____

_____

_____

_____

"Is there another solution?"

_____

_____

_____

_____

"What can I do, or what can I say to find a solution or change the behavior?"

_____

_____

_____

_____

Remember the old myth, "The grass is greener on the other side." Looking to someone else to escape your own issues with your current relationships or situations is only redirecting your problem somewhere else.

Lastly, let's review the things we wrote down in the beginning of this chapter as "LUCK"

And take responsibility for the fact that we put ourselves in the position for luck to be on our side.

What things did you do in order to encounter that luck?

_____

_____

_____

_____

Let's all consider ourselves as "Lucky" all the time....

Simply put, it's not the dress; it's the girl in the dress.

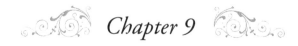

Chapter 9

CONSTRUCTION ZONE

To Do Math, or Not To Do Math ...

When I was younger people thought I was

_____
_____
_____
_____

Because of what happened to me _____, I
felt _____ about myself. Ever since I _____
_____, I've been scared to _____

Ask yourself two questions:
What do I believe about myself to be true?

_____
_____
_____
_____
_____

What do I want to believe about myself to be true?

_____

_____

_____

_____

_____

> "The weak can never forgive.
> Forgiveness is the attribute of the strong."
> -*Mahatma Ghandi*

Think of your beliefs as your own personal city skyline.

Each belief, like a building, stands as tall as you've chosen to build it.

All of the beliefs you have, fill this skyline by your design.

This skyline looks different (just as real ones do) throughout the stages of your life.

The Process:

Step 1: *Pack Your Dynamite*

What do you want to change about yourself?

_____
_____
_____
_____
_____

What do you have to stop believing in order to give this change a chance?

_____
_____
_____
_____
_____

Step 2: *Fire Your Insecurities*
What limiting beliefs do I want to let go of?

_____

_____

_____

_____

Step 3: *Change the Channel*
What or who do I need to stop listening to because they do not empower me?

_____

_____

_____

_____

Step 4: *Close the Recruiting Centre*
What evidence do i need to stop collecting about these limiting beliefs?
Do I need to judge myself less harshly?

_____

_____

_____

_____

Step 5: *Let Yourself Off the Hook*
I will let go of, and forgive myself for:

_____

_____

_____

_____

Step 6: *Delete Old Programming*
It is time to let go of....

_____

_____

_____

Step 7: *Empty the Recycle Bin.*
It is seriously time to let go of:

_____

_____

_____

_____

> "No man is free who is not a master of himself."
> -*Epictetus*

Chapter 10

LOCK AND LOAD

To see yourself as confident, successful and free requires new thought patterns.
How do you see yourself? Time to choose ...

Liking who you are is required. Harnessing your power happens right here--in this space. Spending time to give yourself credit and permission to feel good builds your genuine confidence, fills you with the good kind of pride. This confidence and pride become your protective wear, like armor or Teflon, a force field ... it's like putting on an impenetrable helmet. Deciding what to build next in life when you're protected is an exciting prospect.

> "Make the most of yourself, for that is all there is of you."
> -Ralph Waldo Emerson

Take 5 minutes and write down again all of the wonderful things about you:

_____
_____
_____
_____
_____
_____
_____
_____
_____
_____
_____
_____
_____
_____
_____
_____
_____
_____
_____
_____

Deciding how you see yourself is your responsibility. Becoming the person you want to be starts with a decision to do so. Developing the skills and habits you need to support this new "you" are more easily achieved by following eight basic guidelines:

1. Learn to Lengthen Your Fuse
I will stop reacting to:

_____

_____

_____

I will no longer get upset when:

_____

_____

_____

2. Increase Your Tolerance for Trouble
The reasons I should stay calm are:

_____

_____

_____

3. Develop Your Patience
I will stop making mistakes when I:

_____

_____

_____

4. Expect to Succeed--Success Is a Mindset
Tell yourself you will succeed:

_____

_____

_____

> "If you can't get a compliment any other way, pay yourself one."
> *-Mark Twain*

5. Ask for Confirmation Only from Within
Write down your belief in your abilities, do not lessen this statement because of the opinion of anyone else.

_____

_____

_____

> Close your eyes and ask yourself how you feel. If what you're doing feels right, then embrace it. Say out loud so that you can hear the confidence in your own voice "I can do this," and allow the feeling of confidence to stay with you ... your little secret wing woman.

6. Build on What You Already Know
When have you succeeded before? List those accomplishments, carry them with you.

_____

_____

_____

7. Commit to the Person You Are Becoming
What things can you do to "act as if" you are this new successful you?

_____

_____

_____

8. Discipline Gets You There
Write down what you will do daily to be the person you want to be.

_____

_____

_____

_____

_____

_____

For more tips on presenting the confident person you are, visit us at www.JulieandMichell.com

Rate yourself on a scale from 1 – 10 with 1 being not well and 10 being confident, capable and strong:

How have I seen myself? _____

How do I want to see myself? _____

Question Number Four:

HOW ARE YOU MANAGING YOUR SURROUNDINGS?

Relationships, circumstances, obstacles, and successes are not accidental.

> "We judge ourselves by what we feel capable of doing; others judge us by what we have done."
> *-Henry Wadsworth Longfellow*

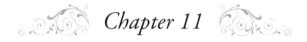

Chapter 11

WHO'S AT YOUR PARTY?

Relationships are not accidental.

Make a list of all the people right now in your life that directly have an impact on the way you feel, and/or on the things you do. This is everyone from the most frustrating and discouraging relationships to the ones you love the most.

Make a list of names.

_____

_____

_____

_____

_____

_____

Law of Resonance

We attract those that are like us

_____

_____

_____

The Head Table

From the names you listed, choose who is at your head table:

_____

_____

_____

_____

What do you appreciate about each one:

_____

_____

_____

_____

What can you do this week to tell them how much we appreciate them?

_____

_____

_____

_____

The Contemplated Guest

From the list, choose which names you are judging or under estimating:

_____

_____

_____

Why are you judging them or underestimating them?

_____

_____

_____

What are their strengths?

_____

_____

_____

What's good about them?

_____

_____

_____

What can you do this week to view them differently and give them benefit of the doubt?

_____

_____

_____

_____

Are you allowing your judgments to stand in the way of a potential great relationship?

Why is this person in my life?

_____

_____

_____

_____

What lessons can I gain?

_____

_____

_____

_____

How may I serve this person?

_____

_____

_____

_____

Why do I feel this way and how do I change that?

_____

_____

_____

_____

_____

_____

_____

_____

Also, decide how much weight this person holds in your life.

_____

_____

_____

The Unexpected Guest
From the list, choose the names of the people that showed up in your life unexpectedly:

_____

_____

_____

_____

What happened when they showed up?

_____
_____
_____
_____

Are you open to allowing others to help you?

_____
_____
_____
_____
_____

In what ways have they aided you?

_____
_____
_____
_____

The Assistant

From the list of names, name the people who have been your mentors: (You may have listed them in another category as well)

_____
_____
_____
_____

How have they assisted you?

_____
_____
_____
_____
_____

How have you assisted them?

_____

_____

_____

_____

_____

_____

The Empty Chair

Now it's time to describe who's missing:

_____

_____

_____

_____

_____

Gardening:

From the list of the names, name the person or people that need to move on from your list:

_____

_____

_____

_____

Why do they need to move on?

_____

_____

_____

_____

Is it a win/win by them moving on?

_____

_____

_____

_____

What actions are you going to take to let go of these relationships?

_____

_____

_____

_____

_____

By releasing and letting go of some of the current relationships that were not working in my life, it created room for exciting new faces.

_____

_____

_____

_____

_____

How are you managing your relationships that have ended?

_____

_____

_____

_____

_____

Are you allowing yourself to let go so that both parties can move on? Managing your surroundings by letting go of that ended relation ship will open the door for exciting new adventures.

How are you managing your surrounding relationships?

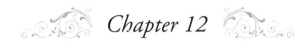

Chapter 12

SNAKES AND LADDERS

Levels and Life

Look at life as though it is lived on a series of levels. Every level has lessons and every experience brings knowledge. This knowledge is required to ascend to levels of new heights... it just doesn't feel that way when you are falling down a level, but it is that way.

List some levels you've climbed in your life:

_____

_____

_____

_____

One of the first ladders I had to climb was:

_____

_____

_____

What this climb taught me was:

_____

_____

_____

_____

I have survived several snakes so far and am proud of myself for it.

> "I have said the words *I am not afraid* many times in my life.
> I have whispered them to convince myself.
> I have spoken them aloud to convince others."
> -Carly Fiorina

What the snakes have taught me:

_____
_____
_____
_____

The next ladder I am climbing is:

_____
_____
_____
_____

The stuff I would have totally screwed up on this last ladder if not for the lessons I had learned from the previous ladders or the snakes are:

_____
_____
_____
_____

I, _____ , choose to view the phases and stages of my career and life as a series of lessons, all intended to serve me in some way to be able to succeed at living and earning the life that I want.

Signed: _____ *Dated:* _____

Chapter 13

NECESSARY EVILS

That "Person"

These are the challenging and disruptive people in our lives.

Who are these people for me?

_____
_____
_____
_____

> "There is no little emeny."
> *-Benjamin Franklin*

That "Place"

It's the slump, the dumps: the place we feel defeated.

Where is this place for me and when does it exist?

_____
_____
_____
_____

That Unpleasant "Thing"

This is an unfortunate set of circumstances, obstacles or accidents, which have caught us off guard.

Mine are:

_____

_____

_____

_____

Recognizing Your Pai Mei

"When the pupil is ready the master will appear". Pai Mei was the kung fu master in the movie "Kill Bill" and brutally tortured his student Beatrix. Because of his brutality, Beatrix learned to be a master herself.

Who is your Pai Mei?

_____

_____

_____

_____

The Law of the Jungle

In the animal kingdom the Lion is the most fierce beast and must outrun the slowest gazelle or it will starve to death. The Lion teaches all animals to run faster than they've ever run before. The Lion is the necessary evil - in this context.

Who is your Lion? (metaphorically speaking).

_____

_____

_____

_____

Why?

_____

_____

_____

_____

_____

_____

"You can't connect the dots looking forward; you can only connect them looking backwards. So you have to trust that the dots will somehow connect in your future. You have to trust in something—your gut, destiny, life, karma, whatever. This approach has never let me down, and it has made all the difference in my life.."
-Steve Jobs in his commencement speech at Stanford, 2005.

What have you gained/learned/experienced as a result of your necessary evils?

_____

_____

_____

_____

_____

Where would you be had you not encountered the above?

_____

_____

_____

_____

_____

Chapter 14

PICK YOUR PERSPECTIVE

Perception is reality.

What if you challenged your surroundings and decided to see an opponent's point of view?

What if everything you think and see is halfway made up because of what you believe to be true?

What if the people that are accusing you of doing something are right?

Answer the questions above based on your current challenging situation.

_____

_____

_____

_____

_____

_____

Could you see things differently if you use another perspective?

_____

_____

_____

_____

My perspective on average changed my life...

> "I consider myself an average man,
> except in the fact that I consider myself an average man."
> -Michel de Montaigne

PERSPECTIVE M.R.I.

Rate yourself from 1-10 indicating your degree of dissatisfaction for each specific category. 1 being happy, confident, feel positive about, and 10 being unhappy, stressed about, fearful of, ashamed etc. Be honest. This is for you.

PHYSICAL WELL BEING		
	SCORE	THOUGHTS
1. Weight		
2. Body Image		
3. Eating Habits		
4. Medical Health		
5. Wardrobe		
6. Image I Project		
7. Fitness Level / Activeness		
8. Energy Level		
9. Sufficient Sleep		
10. Rest Periods / Free Time		
TOTAL / 100		

FINANCIAL HEALTH		
	SCORE	THOUGHTS
1. Debts Being Handled		
2. Bills Being Paid		
3. Spending Under Control		
4. Saving is a Priority		
5. Financial Game Plan in Place		
6. Income Level		
7. Tax Situation		
8. Financial Coaches		
9. Financial Education		
10. Money to Enjoy		
TOTAL / 100		

CAREER / WORK		
	SCORE	THOUGHTS
1. Environment		
2. Relationship with Coach		
3. Addressing Concerns		
4. Manageable Workload		
5. Competent at Tasks		
6. Am in the Right Role		
7. Will Lead to Desired Role		
8. Relationships at Work		
9. Proper Recognition		
10. Career Plan in Place		
TOTAL / 100		

COMMUNICATION		
	SCORE	THOUGHTS
1. I communicate well		
2. I listen with presence		
3. I stay calm in conflict		
4. Not afraid to speak up		
5. I feel heard		
6. I feel understood		
7. I can negotiate		
8. I think before I speak		
9. I can talk about feelings		
10. I can discipline fairly		
TOTAL / 100		

EDUCATION / DEVELOPMENT		
	SCORE	THOUGHTS
1. I am excited to learn		
2. I have a mentor		
3. I make time for learning		
4. I feel personal growth		
5. Time to pursue passions		
6. Money to pursue passions		
7. I feel bored		
8. I do too much		
9. I feel scared to learn		
10. I know how to be happy		
TOTAL / 100		

FAMILY		
	SCORE	THOUGHTS
1. Relationship with mother		
2. Relationship with father		
3. Relationship with children		
4. Relationship with others		
5. Events are a pleasure		
6. Conflicts with parenting?		
7. I feel appreciated		
8. I feel supported		
9. I feel loved		
10. Enough time together		
TOTAL / 100		

FRIENDS		
	SCORE	THOUGHTS
1. Close friend		
2. Close friend		
3. New friends		
4. Old friends		
5. Enough time together		
6. Bad friends still around		
7. Myself as a friend		
8. Friendship to repair		
9. Vacation time with friends		
10. Social events		
TOTAL / 100		

INTIMATE PARTNERSHIP

	SCORE	THOUGHTS
1. We appreciate each other		
2. Openly communicate		
3. Trust		
4. Physical affection		
5. How much I give		
6. How much I receive		
7. Enough time together		
8. Do we fight fair?		
9. Am I happy?		
10. Sex?		
TOTAL / 100		

SPIRITUAL LIFE / COMMUNITY

	SCORE	THOUGHTS
1. Time for self-reflection		
2. Time for meditation		
3. Time for prayer		
4. Involved in community		
5. Feeling of belonging		
6. Time for charity		
7. Connected to inner self		
8. Connected to beliefs		
9. Connected by beliefs		
10. Feel spiritual growth		
TOTAL / 100		

MEANING / INNER PEACE		
	SCORE	THOUGHTS
1. I enjoy time with myself		
2. I can sit still		
3. I can trust my intuition		
4. I trust my future		
5. I feel a higher purpose		
6. I am lonely		
7. I am scared		
8. I feel fulfilled		
9. I listen to myself		
10. I forgive myself		
TOTAL / 100		

TOTALS		
	SCORE	THOUGHTS
1. Physical Well-Being		
2. Financial Health		
3. Career / Work		
4. Communication		
5. Education		
6. Family		
7. Friends		
8. Intimate Partnership		
9. Spiritual Life / Community		
10. Meaning / Inner Peace		
TOTAL / 100		

Thank yourself for just completing the above exercise! Doing a perspective M.R.I. on yourself is a thoroughly intense exploration! Now that you have though, what do you notice? Are you surprised at where the biggest areas of stress are in your life? The biggest areas you want to improve? Which areas you feel good about? Which areas are you most proud of?

_____

_____

_____

_____

_____

_____

_____

_____

Where do you want to spend more time?

_____

_____

_____

_____

What matters the most to you to improve, and what will you do to do that?

_____

_____

_____

_____

Rate yourself on a scale from 1 – 10 with 1 being not well and 10 being extremely well:

How well have I been managing my surroundings? _____

How well would I like to be managing my surroundings? _____

Question Number Five:

HOW WELL DO YOU HANDLE THINGS WHEN YOU FEEL YOU AREN'T WINNING?

What you do when you feel things aren't going your way is a revealing piece in the puzzle.

> "The man who makes no mistakes does not usually make anything."
> *-Edward Phelps*

Chapter 15

TRIGGER-HAPPY

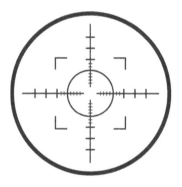

The people who currently have or have had me in their crosshairs are:

_____

_____

_____

_____

_____

I recognize that how I see myself plays a large part in this war zone, and I recognize that at times the result will be beyond my control - A lesson I am meant to survive...

Signed: _____

Survival Tactics 101:
Disarm Your Sniper

1. Stop reacting to their mess. Remove their opinion because you are no longer interested.

   _____

   _____

2. Look in the mirror. Are you partly responsible?

   _____

   _____

3. Stop trying to fix them. Are you? Are you hoping they will change?

   _____

   _____

4. Stop trying to please them. Are you?

   _____

   _____

5. Try to understand them. What's good about them?

   _____

   _____

6. Understand your participation in the relationship. Are you adding to the fuel

   _____

   _____

Maybe you are unintentionally carrying a machine gun ready to fire at someone else's target. The more you judge the person and the more you react negatively, the more it will fuel the fire. Acknowledge your participation. When you shift your thinking to a more positive and understanding state, others tend to shift with you.

When you feel as though you aren't winning, how are you treating others around you?

> When your firing squad realizes that they have no target, they lower their guns.

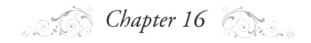 *Chapter 16*

COMFORTABLY UNCOMFORTABLE

Complacency
What parts of your life are feeling complacent?

_____

_____

_____

_____

_____

_____

_____

Groundhog Day
What parts of your life feel like ground hog day? (you know, reliving the same day... day after day after day after day after day)

_____

_____

_____

_____

_____

_____

_____

The Comfort Trap

Settling into dissatisfying situations in your life because you are too reliant on the certainty of the current situation.

Where are the Comfort traps in your life?

_____
_____
_____
_____
_____

Comfortably Uncomfortable

Where are you feeling comfortably uncomfortable?

_____
_____
_____
_____

What are the consequences of remaining where you are?

_____
_____
_____
_____
_____

Changes

What 3 things, if done immediately, would change the current routine?

1. _____
_____
2. _____
_____
3. _____
_____

Who can help you or hold you accountable:

_____
_____
_____
_____

First steps...

_____
_____
_____
_____
_____
_____
_____
_____

"Real integrity is doing the right thing, knowing that nobody's going to know
whether you did it or not."
-Oprah Winfrey

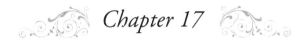

Chapter 17

WAKE-UP CALL

Mine was brutal. Really facing what you think about your life can be one of the toughest things you've ever done. Succeeding at achieving some goals only to realize that you now want different goals can be like driving a truck into a brick wall in sixth gear.

Getting paralyzed as a result of this "crash" for a time, and staying that way, unconscious, because you do not know what to do, that's when a wake-up call occurs... Wake-up calls happen when you leave yourself no other choice ...

The MOST important thing for us to do is often the one thing we are the best at NOT doing:

> "Only do what your heart tells you."
> *-Princess Diana*

So, how do you find your voice? (if its not already shouting at you!)

Ask yourself a few questions:

    1. How are you?

_____

_____

_____

    2. What is good and what is not good?

_____

_____

_____

    3. What do you want to do about that?

_____

_____

_____

These pure and simple questions carry the answers that tell us the truth.

Next:

How do you find the right advisors?

There are two distinct questions we need to ask when we look for an advisor:

    1. Who can teach me what I need to know?

_____

_____

    2. Who will help me feel the way I need to feel?

_____

_____

How do you ask a person to mentor you? Write down what you will say:

_____

_____

_____

_____

_____

_____
_____
_____
_____
_____

Some tips when communicating with a mentor:

1. Be Prepared. Ways I can do this are:

_____
_____
_____
_____
_____

2. Be respectful of time and focus on remaining on task. Ways I can do this are:

_____
_____
_____
_____
_____

3. Leave each session with specific take aways, and things to work on.

When is it that I usually feel I am not winning?

_____
_____
_____
_____

What I will do differently in these situations now:

_____
_____
_____
_____

One step at a time...

What steps will I take next?

_____

_____

_____

_____

_____

_____

_____

_____

_____

_____

"God doesn't give you more than you can handle... my goodness,
He must think the world of me."
-Michell

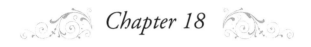

Chapter 18

ATTITUDE ANONYMOUS

I want to get my hopes up...

How many of you can kick serious butt if you really wanted to?

How do you wake up wanting to every day?

Step 1: *Edit your Surroundings*

What things make me feel "less" when I see them?

_____

_____

_____

_____

_____

Step 2: *Talk to Yourself*

What do I say to myself inside my own head? What should I say instead?

_____

_____

_____

_____

Step 3: *Sole Possession of the Remote Control*

_____

_____

_____

What do I listen to?

_____

_____

_____

What do I watch?

_____

_____

_____

What do I read?

_____

_____

_____

How do I escape?

_____

_____

_____

Who else do I allow to influence me?

_____

_____

_____

Step 4: *Always Carry Insurance*
Write a message of encouragement to yourself - from your heart.

_____

_____

_____

Step 5: *Have a Recognition Ritual*

_____

_____

_____

Have a wall of fame somewhere in your life. Do you have one? What should be on it?

_____

_____

_____

Treat yourself. Do you? How would you like to treat yourself?

_____

_____

_____

Plan a reward. What would you love as a reward?

_____

_____

Take time to say thank you. Thank yourself right here - you know what for, write it down.

_____

_____

_____

Step 6: *Look for Others*
Who is a good influence on me? How can I influence them positively too?

_____

_____

_____

_____

_____

> "He who controls others may be powerful,
> but he who has mastered himself is mightier still."
> *-Laozi*

How would you like to start winning again?

Rate yourself from 1 – 10 with 1 being "not well" to 10 being "very well".

How well do you feel you handle things when you aren't winning? _____

How would you like to feel you handle things when you aren't winning? _____

CONVICTION

Question Number Six:
WOULD YOU BET ON YOURSELF TO WIN?

The honesty of this answer is inescapable.
Bet on yourself to win.

> "A lot of people are waiting for Martin Luther King or
> Mahatma Gandhi to come back ---but they are gone.
> We are it. It is up to us. It is up to you.."
> -*Marian Wright Edelman*

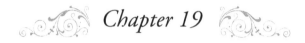
GLADIATOR

When do you feel defeated?

_____
_____
_____
_____
_____

Why?

_____
_____
_____
_____
_____

What are your strengths?

_____
_____
_____
_____
_____

List some major obstacles you have encountered in the past that you had to overcome:

_____
_____
_____
_____
_____

How did you get past them?

_____
_____
_____
_____
_____

Who was there for you?

_____
_____
_____
_____
_____

> "A man whose errors take ten years to correct is quite a man."
> *-J. Robert Oppenheimer*

How can you use some of your past experiences to overcome your current areas of stress?

_____
_____
_____
_____
_____

FIND YOUR GLADIATOR AND RISE AGAIN
The champion lies within...

Become the Gladiator
Visit us at www.JulieandMichell.com

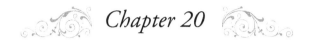 *Chapter 20*

PERSONAL MAGIC

Do you believe in miracles?

_____

_____

_____

What do you believe can happen?

_____

_____

_____

Do you kindle a passion for something more in life?
Describe what this is for you:

_____

_____

_____

Unwrap your gift: Describe what you are naturally gifted or talented at. (Don't you dare say nothing! You know what it is... let it exist, set it free!)

_____

_____

As a child, what hobbies were you drawn to?

_____

_____

_____

As a child, what sports were you drawn to?

_____

_____

_____

As a child, what tv shows or games were you drawn to?

_____

_____

_____

What are you naturally good at?

_____

_____

_____

_____

How can you incorporate these talents and gifts in your current life?

_____

_____

_____

_____

"BUT OF COURSE!"

List out all of the "lucky" things that have happened to you lately:

_____

_____

_____

The very next positive thing that happens to you, say out loud **"But Of Course!!!"**

Chapter 21

COMFORTABLY VULNERABLE

Check next to each one of these that apply to you:

- Are you ever unable to express your emotions?
- Are you sometimes unable to let go of or forgive a past injustice?
- Do you feel overprotective of your personal space?
- Are you ever unable to cry or let others see you cry?
- Do you often hide your true feelings or never let your guard down?
- Do you feel as though you never want to love again?
- Do you sometimes have a hard time trusting others?
- Do you shy away from meeting others for fear of rejection?
- Do you often feel as though you are being judged?
- Do you feel as though some people are trying to take advantage of you?

Define *vulnerable*:

_____

_____

What areas of life are you hiding or not allowing others to see who you are?

_____

_____

_____

What are you attempting to protect?

_____

_____

_____

Why are you avoiding this?

_____

_____

_____

What are you afraid of that people will find out about you?

_____

_____

_____

Why Be Vulnerable?

_____

_____

_____

Check next to each one of these you agree with:
- Being vulnerable first allows others to be okay with being vulnerable too.
- It allows us to let others take the lead, giving us more time for ourselves.
- It enables us to say no.
- Vulnerability builds credibility and trust.
- It allows us to say "I'm sorry" without having to defend and be right every time.
- It introduces us to new people and social circumstances, releases blockages, and opens our minds to new beliefs that may trump our old ones.
- It improves our relationships.
- It allows others around us to understand and feel better about who they are.

From the list, pick your top three that you feel is an area you'd like to work on.

1. _____

2. _____

3. _____

Finding Freedom Within:

Start with some of these steps and practice diligently. Once you find positive results, your confidence will resume and then soar.

1. Be open to receiving.

   _____

   _____

2. Say thank you when someone compliments you. Receive the compliment-- let it in.

   _____

   _____

3. Accept feedback without becoming defensive.

   _____

   _____

4. Allow yourself to be hurt without casting blame or judgement.

   _____

   _____

5. Forgive yourself and be okay with your mistakes.

   _____

   _____

6. Listen to others without feeling the need to give advice.

   _____

   _____

7. Admit when you are sorry.

   _____

   _____

8. Take several risks.

   _____

   _____

9. Try someone else's ideas - other people are smart and creative too.

_____

_____

10. Push yourself to try something new. Say hello to a stranger.

_____

_____

11. Think before jumping to conclusions about other people's motives.

_____

_____

12. Don't be embarrassed to mourn.

_____

_____

13. Be open to a change.

_____

_____

Chapter 22

GET YOUR SWAGGER ON!

THE ZONE:

That place of perfect performance on autopilot. How do you define your "zone"?

_____

_____

_____

_____

When are you in THE ZONE?

_____

_____

_____

_____

_____

How do you get in THE ZONE?

_____

_____

_____

_____

The first steps:

1. Do something! Anything!

_____

_____

2. Turn off all distractions.

_____

_____

3. Be your biggest fan. Tell yourself that you are great.

_____

_____

4. Put on your blinders and focus only on the goal.

_____

_____

5. Tap into your infinite wisdom.

_____

_____

The Eye of the Tiger

What are you're your proudest moments?

_____

_____

_____

_____

_____

Rate yourself on a scale from 1 - 10:

How confidently have you bet on yourself to win in the past? _____

How confidently will you bet on yourself to win now? _____

Now fill out the "Ride of Your Life". On the chart provided on the next page, answer each of the Six Questions on a scale from 1 - 10 (with 1 being the lowest and 10 being the highest). Make a mark on each line indicating your answers.

The Ride of your Life

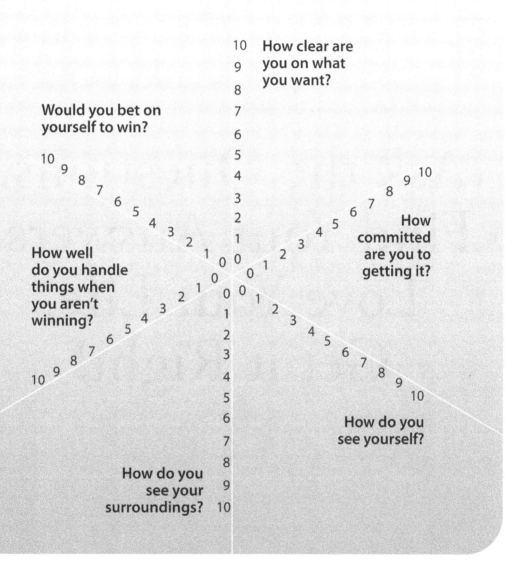

How clear are you on what you want?

Would you bet on yourself to win?

How committed are you to getting it?

How well do you handle things when you aren't winning?

How do you see yourself?

How do you see your surroundings?

After you have indicated your answers, draw a line (like a circle) connecting each of your answers. How does the ride look? How does it feel? How can you make the ride smoother? Could you go faster and farther with less consistent effort if you could make the "tires" bigger in size?

Go back and look at the answers you wrote down at the end of each section throughout the workbook. Using the numbers you assessed at the time of each section close, does this explain some of your past results?

Ask the Questions. Find Your Answers. Love Your Life. Get it Right!

GRATITUDE
ANONYMOUS

> "Gratitude is not only the greatest of virtues, but the parent of all the others."
> *-Cicero*

We have met so many people over the past 17 years. It has been an incredible education. People who have been mentors to us and have taught us incredible lessons, people who we have coached who have taught us incredible lessons, and mostly people who have inspired us to invest in ourselves and each other.

We are very grateful, for our lessons, our perspectives, our teachers and our opportunities. We are grateful for the chance to express our gratitude to everyone who has made a difference in our own lives.

Saying thank you is a privilege and it is a contact sport we intend to fully engage in. Having so many people to say thank you to is extraordinary evidence that wonderful people are indeed everywhere.

Gratitude readings from all who wish to do so...

Who in my life would love some help?
Who can I make a difference to in a very big way?

We invite you to send out some letters – letters of pure gratitude to those in your life that are everyday heroes. Receiving a piece of mail that is not a bill, not a wedding invitation and not for a special occasion gets noticed. Put a smile on someone's face.

You have made a difference in my life. You are someone I appreciate very much....

I Think You are Wonderful.

Although I haven't told you enough, I wanted to tell you now, that all of the thoughtful things you do – I notice and appreciate.

I feel so lucky to have you in my life.

You make a very big difference to me... and I love you for that.

In a world as busy as ours is today sometimes gratitude gets lost in our scheduling challenges... but not today, not for you.

Thank you for all that you do.

To me -you are amazing... and I thought it was time I told you so.

I'm not looking for any thanks in return and so I send this to you... anonymously. ☺

YOU
MAKE A
DIFFERENCE
TO ME

I Feel So Lucky
To Have You In My Life.
You Make Such A Difference,
To So Many People.

Especially Me.

Please visit us at www.JulieandMichell.com for more free tools to use.

Follow us on twitter @JulieandMichell

Like us on Facebook www.facebook.com/JulieandMichell

Until next time,
Julie & Michell

www.JulieandMichell.com

ABOUT THE AUTHORS

Julie Edmonds, entrepreneur, business consultant, and mother of two, founded Strictly Advertising Inc. 17 years ago after her first direct sales job after college. After receiving a BA in Finance from the University of SW Louisiana, she moved to Florida where her entrepreneurial spirit surfaced. Because of her fiercely independent and competitive nature, her business grew to generate gross revenues over one million dollars annually year after year. She has built a large organization of sales offices across the US that currently produces collectively over 8 million in direct sales annually. In 1998 she was featured in Cosmopolitan Magazine as one of 1998's Fun, Fearless, Females, showcasing her business success. Today she operates her consulting company, LNE Consulting, Inc. (*www.lneconsultinginc.com*), founded in 2009. Julie is passionate about coaching and developing young business professionals; she has helped develop and assist thousands to reach professional goals, open their own businesses and take control of their lives.

Michell Smith is a dynamic leadership and management consultant working with one of the largest direct marketing networks across North America. Located in Toronto, Canada, she founded I.C.E. Inc. in September 1996 (www.iceinctoronto.com) and has since built a direct sales network that at its height was comprised of over 60 managers and assistant managers, 600 sales reps and over 10 million dollars in annual revenues. Michell specializes in coaching individuals and teams to reach their highest potential by helping them define their purpose and passion. Today she continues to consult and coach hundreds of entrepreneurs, business owners, students and sales reps all across North America through live seminars and private coaching sessions.

Through their careers, **Julie and Michell** have collectively coached tens of thousands of people and are well respected for their honesty and inspirational voices. They have been committed to the development of people professionally and personally and have both been consistently recognized by their peers with numerous awards for their contributions to the personal success of other entrepreneurs.

Each of them has personally conducted well over 30,000 interviews while recruiting for their sales forces, and between them, they have aided in opening over 200 companies in the past 17 years.

Printed in the USA
CPSIA information can be obtained
at www.ICGtesting.com
JSHW060042150824
68134JS00028B/2598